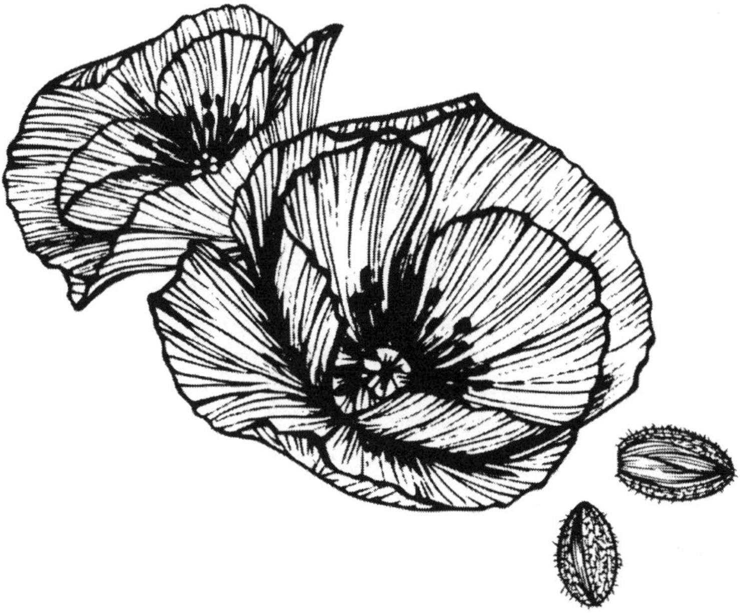

"In the universe, there are things that are known, and things that are unknown, and in between, there are doors."
– William Blake

Prologue

Language, in all its forms, be it spoken or written, transcends dimensions.
What is meant to be personal can be cast as a universal truth and what is meant to be universal can be captured, felt and understood on a deep personal level.
Language is the divine. It lives, it moves, it grows.
Language is what makes us human. It is the spirit pouring out of the body to astral-project into infinity.
Language is how we love and how we destroy.
Relationships are initiated and built through language. Each word like a brick lays the foundation and builds either a home or a wall.
Long before weapons are raised and fired, war is DECLARED through words.
Language connects us to each other, creation and… the creator.
Language connects us to our inner-selves.
Language IS the human experience.
And language reveals who we really are… 'For the world was spoken into creation and we are made in his image'.

Poetry is merely the worship of the divine -The worship of Language.

Prologue **1**

Eclipse (of the self) **10**

In Comparison **11**

Under the Moon **12**

Understanding **13**

That which is Hidden **14**

Our Reflection **15**

Untold **16**

Ironic **17**

Solipsism **18**

The Moon and the Stars **19**

The Divine Tragedy **20**

Conversations with the Moon **21**

Animus & Anima **22**

Symphony of the Universe **23**

In between **24**

Unknown **25**

Small **26**

Mother Nature's Ethos **27**

The Abyss **28**

Head over heels **30**

Tethered Line **31**

The Moon and the Tide **32**

Not star-crossed **33**

Innate **34**

Chemistry **35**

Glitch **36**

Intertwined **37**

Starry Sky **38**

Green Eyes **39**

Your Hands **40**

Good Morning **41**

Soiled **43**

Seasonal **44**

Fragile **45**

Confused **46**

The Match **47**

Stop! **48**

Apologize **49**

Sign **50**

Remember Me Not **51**

Stale **52**

Careless **53**

If words are my weapon, then silence is my armour **54**

Bitter **55**

Dust **56**

Growing Up **58**

Castles in my mind **59**

Careless **60**

Where do I fall? **61**

Waves **62**

Mosaic **63**

Septet of Deadly Sins **64**

Night Time Sirens **65**

Far too Long **66**

Silence Speaks **67**

Art of Forgiveness **68**

Nu-Metal **69**

Spiraling **70**

My Talisman **71**

Pieces of Me **72**

Why the rib? **73**

Phoenix **74**

Briars **75**

December **76**

Childhood **77**

Torrid Longing **78**

Just to Provoke **79**

Shadow **80**

Avoidance **81**

Societal Antigen **82**

Will it matter? **83**

You Never Listen **84**

My Friends Don't Like Me **85**

Hypocrite **86**

Sly **87**

The Reason I write **88**

Beauty in Decay **89**

Fool **90**

Loudspeaker **91**

Brain eating Amoeba **92**

Envy **93**

Tap the Toad **94**

Like an Oyster **95**

He Said **96**

Tumble **97**

Sepia **98**

Hope is a Heavy Thing to Carry **99**

Poetry Falls **101**

Rivers of Me **102**

Frankenstein Scars **103**

Shoreline of My Mind **104**

Demeter **105**

A wonderfully awful place **106**

Magic and Rainbows? **108**

Naiveté **109**

Soliloquy **110**

Moonlit Conversations **111**

Red Flag **112**

Everblue i **113**

Thought **114**

Withering Flower **115**

Everblue ii **116**

Stygian Sky **118**

Murmurations of sky and sea **119**

African Sunset **120**

Rain, Rain **121**

Winter **122**

Autumn **123**

Rainy Days **124**

Setting **125**

Visitor **126**

Tranquil dawn **127**

The moon and the stars

Eclipse (of the self)

It is only when darkness completely covers
The light, that the halo is revealed.

In Comparison

I have a favorite part of the day:
When the sky summons the moon
And blue and orange halos cascade
Over the horizon, in unison.

The air suddenly becomes crisp
And clear-
I gulp it up and it refreshes my soul.
The moon rises and litters
The sky with glitter
To remind me how small I am
And how small my problems are in
Comparison.

Under the Moon

I am over and under
The moon.
I am soothed
By the sound of thunder.
You remind me
Of tranquil water,
But not for the beauty
Of tranquility,
Rather the mystery
That lies beneath.
You are the quiet
Before the storm.
I am the breeze
That turns into a gale…

Because I love to
Dance in the rain.

Understanding

To understand –
To stand under
A new moon sky
And wonder
What is being
Whispered by the wind.
To hear it in the thunder,
But knowing
To question it is sin.
The heart who has
Understanding
Seeks knowledge,
And knowledge leads
To undoing.

That which is Hidden

The moon shines upon us
And illuminates
All that we wish
To hide.
It's only in the dark
That our deepest
Selves come to light.

Our Reflection

We look up at the night sky
And see a hundred billion stars
Looking back at us,
While a hundred billion neurons
Flicker in our minds,
Unaware that we are looking
At our own reflection.

Untold

The blue canvas of stars
Are light-years of promises
Always out of reach.
They paint a picture
Worth a thousand words
Without an utterance…

A story untold.

Ironic

It's not gravity
That holds the
Universe together,
But rather irony...
Billions of stars
And galaxies,
But we are the only
Only ones capable
Of comprehending
The unfathomable
But we don't...

Solipsism

Am I a whole constellation
Trapped in a container?
I am consciousness
That is all I know.

The Moon and the Stars

I'm lucid dreaming my way through life,
Head up in the clouds,
Feet, rarely on the ground.
Blissfully, I'd rather not open up my eyes,
I'd much prefer to avoid reality,
Thanks!
I dream in rhymes
And notes
And hues and think about simpler times
Of me and you
And the stars
And the moon
The view is much better
From up here...

From afar.

The Divine Tragedy

Perhaps my head aches,
Because the universe is expanding.
Perhaps my heart aches,
Because it longs for understanding.

Perhaps my eyes hurt
From staring at the intricate tapestry
Of life and love and the nature
Of being – The Divine Tragedy.

Conversations with the Moon

Some words can only be
Silently whispered by the soul.
Words hold the power of creation
And therefore the power to undo.
Some words should never be uttered
Except in silent
Conversations with the moon.

Animus & Anima

I have multiple faces,
As the moon has
Multiple phases.
You hide your doubts
As the sun hides
Behind clouds.
You rise and fall like the sun
I pull and tug like the moon
We are *Animus & Anima*
Vying harmoniously
Bound together in orbit.

Symphony of the Universe

Witness the symphony
In the universe
The flight of the Valkyries
As meteors fly by,
Jupiter's swirling
Crimson conduction
Of *Mozart's 41*,
Or the deafening silence
Of a supernova.
Witness the violence
Witness the harmony.

In between

I live somewhere between
The sky and the moon,
The fallen leaf and the forest floor,

A secret and a declaration.

Unknown

I used to think
That it was possible to know,
To understand...
To comprehend the unknown...
The mysteries...
The esoteric nature
Of our existence,
The true purpose of all these complexities.
I sometimes feel it,
Like a word stuck on the tip of my tongue,
An overwhelming realization of something,
Something that can be felt, but never uttered,
Never fully understood...
Just glimpses
Of small puzzle pieces
That make up a bigger picture
That has never been seen
By any mere
Mortal being.
Now I doubt, that I know,
Or can ever know
That which is
Unknown.

Small

I always end up feeling dizzy,
When looking up at the night sky,
To wish upon a distant star -
Like gravity is crushing me.
The weight of the milky way
Slowly bearing down
Reminding me how small I am…
How my light will fade
Before ever reaching back
Across the dark expanse,
Never having the chance
To be wished upon.

Mother Nature's Ethos

As above ...so below
The cornerstone of all we know.
Only light can reveal the shadow.
The wind creates an undertow.
The dark horizon births a new sun.
We find the cure within the poison.
We find the answer within the question,
And our reflection up in the heavens.
Order stems from chaos -
Mother Nature's ethos.

The Abyss

Born from the abyss.
A deep darkness.
The foundation
Of all creation.
The source from
Which all light emerges.
The same abyss
That serves as a canvas
For starlit encrypted
Messages that
Captivate our gaze.

Born from the abyss
A deep darkness.
The fountain
Of consciousness,
From which
Enlightenment
Emerges.
The same abyss
Buried deep in
The back of my
Mind, that I seek
And hide from
At the same time.

You and me

Head over heels

It's magical
The way I fell,
Head over heels,
Heart over head,
Head over heart,
I tumbled
Right into your arms.

Tethered Line

You knew my soul first,
Before we ever met
You were already well-versed
In the language of my head.

Your eyes recognized mine
A mirror back twin,
A tethered line
Embedded deep within.

The Moon and the Tide

I love the sinuous
Ripples each of your words form
On the surface of
My tempestuous ocean
- like the moon and the tide.

Not star-crossed

We are not star-crossed.
The stars aligned just for us.
Times and *Fates* conspired,
Weaving our threads
Across multiple lifetimes.
We have loved and lived
In many forms.
I was once the moon
And you were once the sea.
You were once the wind
When I was but a leaf.
It matters not
the what or when;
Serendipity always
Leads you back to me.

Innate

Captivated by your gaze
T'was love at first sight
The gravitational hold
Impossible to escape
The chemicals react
Irreversible. Fate
Entangled by your ways.
The things you say.
The things you don't
And wish you would.
Ensnared by something innate.

Chemistry

Wide eyed, mesmerized –
Fireworks shooting in my mind.
Images of us
Scrawled across synapses –
Chemical magnum opus.

Glitch

You are comfort – like marshmallows in a mug
You bore me with endless tidbits about dirt bikes.
You are overwrought – like a glazed doughnut.
You annoy me – turbulent back and forth sway of emotions.
You are the best and the worst part of my day.
Your love is a glitch I can live with.

Intertwined

I am you
And you are me.
Together
We are infinitely more
Than we could be
Separately.

Starry Sky

The city lights melted away
Into the starry sky
As the world
Slowly
Faded away,
Until there was
Nothing but
You and I.

Green Eyes

I rarely listen to what you have to say.
Your curated words are a curtain
And the poet in me needs to peek
Behind the layer.
I rarely listen to the words,
 But I hear every motive and
Intention and I look for truth
In your green eyes that
Slant into music
When they reveal that
Which you so carefully conceal
From the rest of the world…
Your heart.

Your Hands

When we first met,
I remember looking at your hands
Folded together in front of you -
In front of me -
Between us.
Your hands have touched,
Every part.
Your hands have stained
My heart.
They leave a print, a residue
A glue, that bonds
Me to you.

Good Morning

Amber rays through the window
Wake me at dawn.
They cascade over your arm
That is draped across my body.
I look out of the window to see
That the sky is on fire
Just like the wildfire
In my heart.

Love and all its complexities

Soiled

A white shirt is lying on the floor,
You said it would look better there,
But you lied about a lot of things
That shirt just like my innocence
Has now been soiled
By you.

Seasonal

She's seasonal like summer.
During her absence
You feel the cold sting of
Regret and loneliness.
During your barren winter
You miss her presence
And the warmth of
Her eyes when she smiles.
You forget all about
The miseries that summer
Brings with its
Scorching heat and
Repression of rain.
You long for summer
Even though it only
Brings you pain.

Fragile

Take it easy on me,
I am more fragile
Than you think.
Careful with those
Razor edged words
That you hurl,
Even the smallest cut
Hurts.

Confused

She's a Band-Aid.
She's a blister.
She's a nightmare.
She's a daydream.
I bet you can't help
But miss her.

The Match

How do you know these ashes are mine?
If you look at them
Are you able to see some sort of
Resemblance?
As you dust them up
Do they fill the air with a familiar odor?
Are you overcome with nostalgia
As you place them in an urn (or a bin)?
Or is it
Because you lit the match
And watched me burn?

Stop!

I want to get off this
Merry go round.
I need it to stop
Before I vomit
The words I've been
Swallowing back down,
But round and round
We go!

Apologize

The words I wish to hear?
How about:
'I'm sorry my dear.
Sorry for all the times
I didn't listen
I didn't hear.'
How about:
'I'm sorry I ignored
Your tears
And minimized
Your hopes
And fears.'
How about:
'I'm sorry.'
Plain simple and clear

Sign

If you were waiting for a sign
Wouldn't my silence suffice?
I could have spelled it out for you,
But the part of me that cared
Only knows how to spell...
I n d i f f e r e n c e

Remember Me Not

Remember me not
For the broken promises,
The secrets kept
And
The words unsaid.
Remember me not
For the times I was honest
With words I should have kept
And messages I left unread.
Remember me not
As
The ghost of lover's past.
Remember me not
Not
At all.

Stale

Stale bread has a smell that stings,
That reminds me of stale relationships.
Just like stale bread,
It can sometimes be somewhat
improved with a bit of heat
And just like stale bread toast,
If overdone,
All you are left with is blackened crumbs.

Careless

I have been careless in a different sense.
Not by misplacing keys, being forgetful
Or absent minded.
This matter is much more serious.
I have been careless at your expense;
Misplacing my affection, being forgetful of
Your needs and desires.
I have been careless with your heart
For that I am at fault.

If words are my weapon, then silence is my armour

You say I'm cold
And indifferent,
I'm not,
I'm simply silent.
I have conceded,
Although there will be
No white flag.
The taste of victory
Has become bitter and stale.
I have no interest
In winning-
I have no interest in peace.
I am simply silent,
I concede.
You can wage your war,
You can take all the spoils.
You can call yourself victor
And wear your cruelty
Like a badge of honour...
While I
Remain silent....

Bitter

As sweet as honey,
As bitter as bile.

Your words are candy floss clouds
That leave a bitter taste in my mouth.

Dust

My heart turned to dust
the moment you said goodbye.
Then my soul slowly
evaporated, leaving
Nothing but an empty shell.

Bliss and strife

Growing Up

Growing up
I fell more…
And more…
Apart.
The pieces that I thought
Had fit
Suddenly
Became jagged
And rough
And no matter how hard
I tried
I could never get them
Aligned.
So I simply gave up.
Now I just drag them
Along
And pretend to be whole.

Castles in my mind

Unable to grasp,
the sands of time simply slip
right through my fingers.
So I build a sand castle
out of memories instead.

Careless

A careless heart embedded
In a burdened soul,
Wrestles with want and need;
What I need I care not for,
What I want torments my soul.

Where do I fall?

Where do I fall when night comes?
As the sun sets I spiral
Into insanity.
The day is lost with all its day to days
And as daylight fades
I enter the realm of dreams
And endless possibilities.
My mind flickers with the moonlight
And delves deep into an endless
Abyss
That pillows my head
Till morning comes.

Waves

We exist in waves.
We are tragically transient.
Just as waves crash
And return to undulating,
We experience, feel or understand
And then simply return to
Just being.

Mosaic

Memories: treasures forgotten of-
Some of cotton candy,
Some painful,
Some magical,
All together
Tell of a wonderful
Intricate life led
By a nucleic creature-
An incarnate mosaic.

Septet of Deadly Sins

I must confess in virtue_ true to my nature.
From which I cannot waver. That I indulge –
Easily swayed to plunge – in which I must not.
Not in revelry nor thought. But forbidden fruit
Even a taste minute – seems to taste sweeter.
The shade under the cedar – sedative, soothing
Though it leads to undoing – in *Eden* I'll stay.

Night Time Sirens

Night time sirens sing so sweetly.
A sweet lullaby in the dead of night.
I hear them as the wind chimes
And the crickets play their melody
On their stiff leathery wings.
I hear them softly whisper to me
Through the rustling of the leaves.
They keep me awake all night
And I wonder often times
Why must sleep evade me?

Far too Long

Fleeting moments
Turned
Faded memories
I cling to both
I hold on
For far too long.

Silence Speaks

Silence speaks:
A cold glare or a warm smile –
Both equally more capable
Of revealing the truth
Than words ever could.

Art of Forgiveness

The art of forgiveness
Is more similar to
The art of war
Than one would think-
If the act of rushing into
Battle is to admit defeat.

Nu-Metal

It's just one of those days..

Where it feels like my life is one fire
And instead of dousing the flames
I feel like a pyromaniac
Who just wants to watch it burn!

Spiraling

More often than not
I find myself
Spiraling
Into madness,
Fixation,
Depression,
It is always
One or the other.
It starts of slow,
But I'm always
Too late
To catch myself
Before the downward take.

My Talisman

Words – my talisman.
The words I conjure up
Ward off evil and
Possess magical powers
To heal and reveal my heart.

Pieces of Me

Pieces of me are scattered about my home
I hear their little feet
Pitter patter
I look on as they stray
Farther and father
Into the unknown – away
I worry as they need me less and less
Although I know
That this is life's way
Of building more
With pieces
That belonged to me
Once before.

Why the rib?

He was formed from dust
Carefully crafted by clay
Perfect in all ways
Except one -
He was alone.
So from his chest
She was separated.
Formed from the part
That was meant to armor
His heart.

Phoenix

Dust yourself off
Like the phoenix
You are.
Rise with renewed
Conviction from the
Pile of ashes
Where they left you to burn.

Briars

Past promises are
The briars that bind us and
Keep us trapped in a
Prison of nostalgia and
Regret over what was not.

December

It rained all that December,
And washed away our woes.
When the skies finally cleared
A new light emerged,
A renewed spark within.

Childhood

My favorite place,
Has Lego brick walls,
A green carpet of grass,
A garden hose to drink from
Instead of a faucet,
A pillow fort to lie in,
Instead of a bed
And a teddy bear to hold,
Instead of a pillow.
It is a place of wonder and whimsy;
A place only found in memory.

Torrid Longing

I feel it deep down in my soul.
A heartrending convulsion,
A torrid longing for home.
A place only in imagination,
Born in the deepest crevasse
Of my consciousness-
Not real but with more
Sustenance…
Unreachable, except in dreams.

Just to Provoke

I write poetry, not songs.
I write bitter words
Strung together by thoughts
Aimed at striking a chord.
I write about uncomfortable truths
Instead lulling with you comfort.
I sometimes wish I were able to soothe
But I write to cleanse the palate,
To provoke thought,
To loosen the yoke,
Or perhaps...
      Just to provoke.

Shadow

Desolate desolation-
Tautologuous...
Redundant,
But so is loneliness
And isolation...
Sollioquous seclusion
Is where the self
Meets the self.
The shadow seeks not company
Only courage.

Avoidance

There is an abandoned,
Desolate landscape in the back of my mind
I try to avoid it
It scares me
As all abandoned places do
Who knows what has been
Left behind
Memories
Resentment
Hopes and dreams
That never came to be
I try to avoid it
But somehow
Late at night
I always end up there…

Societal Antigen

Mental illness fascinates me-
I romanticize it.
Each archetype
A perfect specimen
Of rebellion,
Fueled by frustration
With the social paradigm.
Perhaps it is not an illness,
Perhaps it is the mind's
Immune response
To a societal antigen.

Will it matter?

Will it matter in the end?
The heavy load that I burdened
The sacrifices I suffered
The hurt?
When the momentous montage
Appears
Will there be a climatic
Plot twist where
Everything suddenly
Make sense
Through a prismatic lens
Of retrospection
In the twilight
Of consciousness
Will there be any perception
Of the finality
Of this existence
Or will it end in a cliffhanger
With the hope of a sequel.

You Never Listen

You ask, but never listen.
You assume and
Carefully
Lay out your
Flawed assumption,
As if it is a riddle that
You finally solved.
With a proud grin
You eagerly wait for
Me to agree,
But I cannot.
 So forgive my silence
And please do
Take it
As a sign
Of indifference.

My Friends Don't Like Me

My friends don't like me, I'm awkward and strange.
I turn into a cold statue when they try to hug me.
I laugh when I'm not supposed to- and don't when I am.
I never know how to respond to "How are you?
I overshare and under-share.
I am impossible to read and yet my face betrays me.
My friends don't like me, but I'm pretty sure they care.

Hypocrite

Your hypocrisy revolts me.
Your forked tongue smile
Barely conceals
The cowardice that
Hides behind your
Grit teeth.
I see how your eyes
Survey your surroundings
For looks of approval.
I see the satisfaction
On your face,
Once you've had your fix.
You're smoke and mirrors
And I see
Right
Through
You.

Sly

You think you are sly,
Like a serpent,
But I see you quiver
Like the coward
You are.
You have more in common
With your slithering friend
Than you think.
Crawl back into
Your hole
Where you belong.

The Reason I write

I am compelled to put my thoughts to paper;
A bloodletting of sorts.
Sometimes I bleed liquid gold,
Sometimes I bleed ink,
Sometimes I bleed bile.
Whether the page is soiled or
Seemingly divinely inspired…
Both are needed to be written
Both are needed to be read.

Beauty in Decay

There something beautiful in decay;
The way that what is no longer needed
Simply withers, dies and falls away
So that what remains becomes seeded.
Take the fallen leaf, coarse and brittle,
Separated forever from its host
The tree, without its leaves, feeling little,
Feeling bare - to the elements exposed.
The stark contrast of death and decay
Masterfully painted by the seasons,
Patiently demonstrate,
Why we suffer –
the reason.

Fool

Barely…
I am barely holding it all together.
I am stuck,
   I am unable to loosen the tether.
I am stuck
In a mediocre production,
Playing the part of the fool.
 So I keep juggling
   And I keep struggling
To keep all the balls in the air.
 I let them drop and I am
Quickly reminded,
That a jester is supposed
To be able to juggle…
Juggle fool,
Juggle!

Loudspeaker

To the loudspeaker
In the center of my cranium...
Shhhh!
Be still – just let me be.
(where is the off switch?)
Let me fail,
Let me stumble,
Just stop criticizing me!
You're too loud,
 You drown out
All logic and reason
With blaring emotion
And magnify
Every misstep,
Every mistake.
Shhhh!
Quiet down
And let me be.

Brain eating Amoeba

Self-doubt-
The brain eating amoeba
That has housed itself
In my skull.
It chews away
Slowly
Savoring
Every last thought,
Or idea,
Not even leaving behind
A morsel that I can cling
Onto.

Envy

Evermore it lingers
Near, never far,
Vehemently
Yearning for more.

Yielding to none,
Virtuous vice
Named
Envy.

Tap the Toad

I am going off on a trip! Off I go
To the space deep inside my head.
There I find the most marvelous of shows;
Orchestrated chaos - nirvana ahead.
I tread carefully and take the eight steps
'Till I reach the hill of enlightenment.
(confused) It is not what you would expect.
I was hoping for some sort of guidance!
I tap the twitching toad to the right:
"You said everything would be alright."

Like an Oyster

Just like an oyster, I will swallow
All adversities that drift into my life
And encase them deep within in my soul,
Until they are polished and refined
And emit a soft luminous glow
That reveals the hope that lies in strife.

He Said

There is a reason
He said, "Let the children
Come to me."
For they are the best
Of us,
Not yet jaded,
Still untainted.
Pure and innocent
Therefore there is no
Forgiveness
No deliverance
For those that harm
A child.

Tumble

During a late night conversation
I wove together a string of thought,
But kept pulling at it afterwards.
Thoughts tangled together
Kept tumbling out of my mind
And all the threads wove together.
The more I tried to untangle the knots
The more unraveled I became.

Sepia

She sings her own song,
An out of sync melody.
She dreams in monochrome
Colourless visions of entropy.

Hope is a Heavy Thing to Carry

Sometimes things are better left unsaid -
Hope is a heavy thing to carry.
Some things have to be felt,
Like grief, heartbreak or regret.

A kind word isn't always kind -
Hope is a heavy thing to carry.
The truth is a cruel gift,
But the recipient is left with a sound mind.

The self

Poetry Falls

Poetry falls from
My lips like an endless stream.
Peaceful and serene,
The weight of my words slowly
Evaporates into mist.

Rivers of Me

I am made of rivers
Some tranquil
Some turbulent
Some lead into valleys
Some lead to the sea
But all of them find
                Their way back to me.

Frankenstein Scars

My skin is engraved with a thousand tales.
Some are illustrated and easy to read,
Painted and scrawled in jet black ink.
Some were never intended
 but tell of a life lived.
  Frankenstein scars - Stitched memoirs.

Shoreline of My Mind

The shoreline of my mind
Is littered with debris.
Broken parts of thoughts,
That sunk into
The deepest trench
Of my consciousness,
Sometimes
Float
Up
And then wash out,
When the tide rises.

Demeter

I hate small talk
I'm not good at it -
Talking small, I mean.
It is difficult to summarize
My existence in a simple phrase.
How am I?
I am paradoxical concoction
Of poison and remedy.
The moon is my closest friend,
Because although,
I understand people
I have never understood
One single person.
It's all too complicated
For me to be able
To express it simply.
So to answer your question:
I just am... Whatever that means.

A wonderfully awful place

The world is a wonderfully awful place.
Whimsical and horrific-
You never know what you'll find.
Friend or foe, snare or embrace?
The world is a wonderfully awful place.
Terrifying or terrific?
The best we can all hope for
      Is to give and receive grace.

Tread Carefully

My garden is filled with foxglove
And nightshade.
Tread carefully
This is not a place
For those who are easily frayed.

Magic and Rainbows?

You see what you think is innocence,
You see what I allow you to see.
You see magic – you see possibility
My smile hides the true nature
Of things...
Magic and rainbows? You forget
That bright colors caution!
How badly do you want it?
How badly do you want to be poisoned?

Naiveté

My constant companion stays.
Unwelcome.
In all the years gone by,
It has not strayed

Soliloquy

A cat smoking a cigarette asks me,
If it speaks would it be soliloquy.
I guess not, the cat IS speaking to me.
Not in rhymes nor riddles, but just plainly.
So therefore it is not soliloquy.
It is utter madness, obviously,
To be thinking that a cat is speaking
To me- or itself. So I keep thinking
And ask the cat if I might be dreaming.
The cat asks me if I should be blinking.

    I kill the cigarette – decide to sleep
    But I can't stop thinking about that creep

Moonlit Conversations

Forged by moonlit conversations,
Tears of disappointment, pillow hugs,
And resolved reflections staring back
At me in my mirror.

Red Flag

My intentions? Unclear
A mystery... even to me
I am complicated you see
I am childish, but I am infinitely wise
If you lend me your ear
I will whisper to you sacred knowledge
I'm a sage
But
Its best not to leave me
To my own devices. I am
As unpredictable as a toddler
I'm childish, I'm wise
I'm complicated
Take me as I am
Or stop
At the red flag.

Everblue i

I am evergreen
Although seasons change
I remain the same.

I am everblue
Lingering luminous supernova
Bursting into hues.

Thought

I was sober of thought for a minute,
Almost remembered who I was...
Who I was before all the criticism and complaints,
Before all of my insecurities took hold.
I almost remembered, but then thought took back control.

Withering Flower

I was not meant for this world.
In another time, or realm,
I would have been revered.
But here I am an outcast;
Condemned to a perpetual
Salem that seeks to snuff
Out my delicate soul.
Here I am but a withering flower
Bound to an icy wasteland.

Everblue ii

Caught by a current,
Drifting in and of melancholy.
The tone, the setting, the mood:
Evermore… *Everblue*.
Lost, without a paddle
Floating on the waves of the abyss…
Wishing I knew
Why I am always… *Everblue*

Seasons and weather

Stygian Sky

The nimbostratus
Floats across the stygian sky,
But I have not a penny to give
To the howling ferryman.

Murmurations of sky and sea

I sat quietly
And my thoughts spiraled.
I thought about
The swirling dance
Of schools of fish
And how they mimic
The pirouette of flocks of
small birds in the sky...
And the universe asked me
"Do you see it, now?
The symmetry...
The harmony...?"

African Sunset

Eternal dusk,
An ominous glow,
The perfect lighting
For my thoughts to flow.
The perfect space to cast a
Shadow between light and dark.

Rain, Rain

Rain, rain please don't go away
Stay until some other day
Fill the air with petrichor
Grime the sky with your visca
Let your living water
Paint in every color
Evergreen and crimson bright
Grey and blue and every hue
So that every canvas may delight

Rain, rain stay for a while
Your grey sky soothes my smile.

Winter

I have a love hate relationship
With winter-
More hate than love.
But I do appreciate
The melancholic
Monochromatic
Beauty of the dry dead
Landscape.
The barren branches
Look like
Finger tips
Holding up the sky,
In a spectacular feet of balance.
But the shiver
Shakes me awake
From my trance,
To remind me that
I'm cold and I hate winter-
Even with all its whimsy.

Autumn

Russet and gold embers fallen from a branch
Rustle underneath my toes with every step
A fiery landscape – monochromatic maze
A cemetery for leaves – summer time's death bed

Rainy Days

The sky is specter grey –
My monotone muse
Mimics my monotone mood
I feel most like myself
On overcast, rainy days.

Setting

Setting
And atmosphere
The sun setting creates
The most perfect atmosphere
And setting.

Visitor

I came home to find
A visitor on my roof
An omen, a sign
I ignored my
Unwelcome guest
Hoping that it would fly
Away and find
Some other house
To harass
But alas
It stayed
For as long as it stayed
My mind would not rest
The thoughts
Were relentless
Thoughts of life
And death
I made a big fuss
And chased it away
It flew into the woods
Into the unknown abyss.

Tranquil dawn

Tranquil dawn
Grey skies and a light breeze
Rustling through elephant grass
While a red-chested cuckoo is
calling the rain
Perfect ambience
For my cacophony of thoughts.

Other titles by the author:

OVERTHOUGHT

Available on amazon

Printed in Great Britain
by Amazon